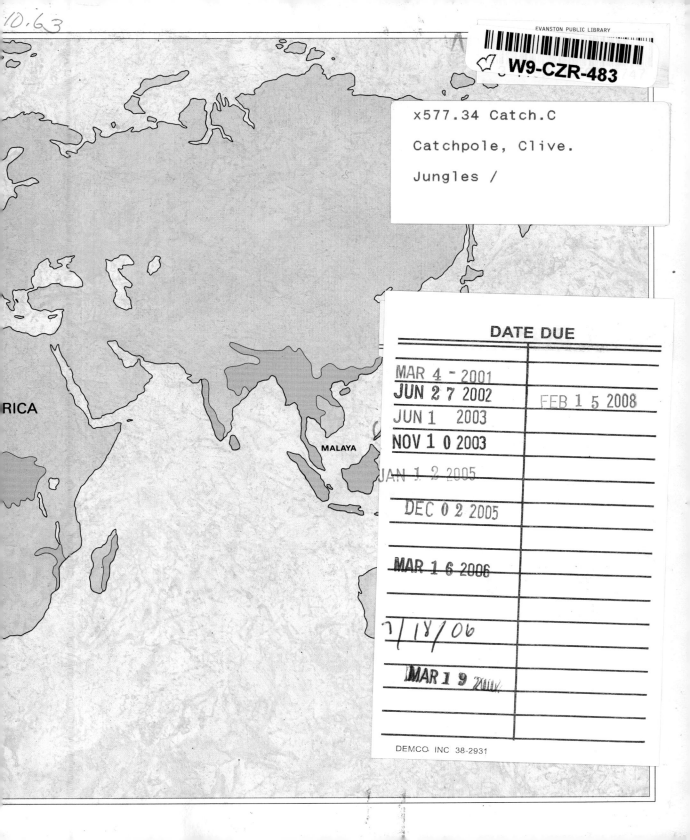

10.63

RICA

MALAYA

For Nicola   C.C.

For James   D.F.

First published in the United States 1984
by Dial Books for Young Readers
A Division of E. P. Dutton, Inc.
2 Park Avenue
New York, New York 10016
Published in Great Britain by Walker Books Ltd.

Printed in Italy
First Edition
10 9 8 7 6 5 4 3 2 1

Library of Congress Cataloging in Publication Data
Catchpole, Clive. Jungles.
Summary: Text and illustrations present the
many beautiful and unusual forms of life
that thrive in the jungle.
1. Jungle ecology—Juvenile literature.
[1. Jungles.] I. Finney, Denise, ill. II. Title.
III. Series.
QH541.5.J8C37 1984   574.5'2642   83-7796
ISBN 0-8037-0034-2

THE LIVING WORLD
JUNGLES

By Dr. CLIVE CATCHPOLE
Pictures by DENISE FINNEY

DIAL BOOKS FOR YOUNG READERS
E. P. Dutton, Inc.   NEW YORK

Jungle is the name commonly given to a
tropical rain forest. Found only near the
equator, where there is plenty of sun as well
as lots of rain, its warm, humid climate
enables plants to grow extremely tall.
Valuable timber is contained within its
bounds, which in turn produces rubber,
cocoa, fruit, nuts, oils, spices, and even rare
drugs. Over half of all the different plants
and animals known exist nowhere else.
Marvelously lush and colorful, the jungle
is teeming with life.

Yet for some plants, growing conditions in the jungle are not as ideal as they might seem. Big trees block out precious sunlight that smaller plants also need in order to thrive. These smaller plants have had to develop ways to survive; jungle orchids and climbing vines, known as lianas, may actually sprout in the bits of dust on upper branches of a tree so as to be closer to the sunlight. Jungle flowers have bright colors and strong scents to attract pollinating insects in the forest gloom.

Life cycle of a
passion flower butterfly

Egg

Caterpillars

Some jungle insects are capable of destroying beautiful flowering plants. Butterflies, for example, may lay eggs on a plant's leaves, and when the eggs hatch, the caterpillars that emerge will eat them. Certain passion flowers have poison in their leaves that prevents this from happening. But there are also certain butterflies that lay eggs only on passion flower leaves. Their caterpillars are immune to the poison, which they store and pass over to the adult butterflies. With this poison the butterflies are protected from being preyed upon by birds, who learn that butterflies with a specific coloring taste unpleasant.

Ready to pupate

Pupa, or chrysalis

Adult butterfly emerging

Only a few such insects contain poisons and are brightly colored so that predators will recognize them and know to stay away. Others rely instead on camouflage to fool the larger animals that try to hunt them. With bodies that look just like twigs, or wings that resemble leaves, they can blend into their jungle background by staying perfectly still. But there are also some hunting insects that use camouflage. A praying mantis from Malaya is invisible against the flower it rests on, and when unsuspecting insects alight, they are snapped up.

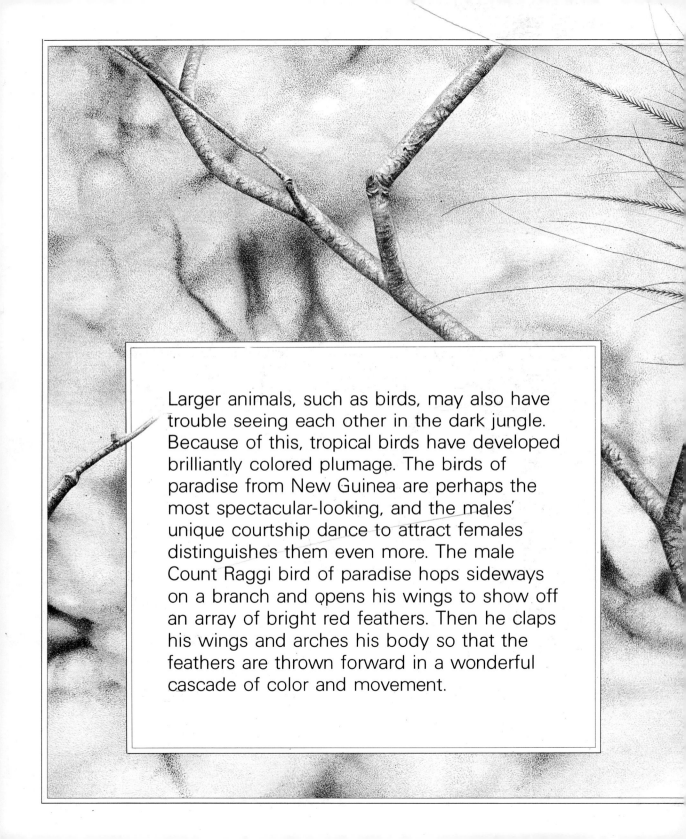

Larger animals, such as birds, may also have trouble seeing each other in the dark jungle. Because of this, tropical birds have developed brilliantly colored plumage. The birds of paradise from New Guinea are perhaps the most spectacular-looking, and the males' unique courtship dance to attract females distinguishes them even more. The male Count Raggi bird of paradise hops sideways on a branch and opens his wings to show off an array of bright red feathers. Then he claps his wings and arches his body so that the feathers are thrown forward in a wonderful cascade of color and movement.

The male satin bowerbird of New Guinea and Australia also has a most unusual courtship ritual to attract a female in the gloom of the forest floor. First he builds a special structure, or bower, from twigs and then decorates it with flowers, feathers, and shiny insects. He may even brighten the walls by painting them with a mixture of saliva and berries. When a female passes by, he tries to entice her by picking out a "bouquet" and doing a dance in front of his colorful bower.

There are many different birds searching for
food in the jungle. Some feed on only one
type of plant and have uniquely shaped bills
to aid them in procuring their meals. For
example, tiny hummingbirds use their long
thin bills to drink nectar from jungle flowers,
which they also pollinate in return. South
American parrots use their strong bills to
crack open Brazil nuts, and the toucan's large
bill is ideal for picking and slicing up soft
jungle fruits.

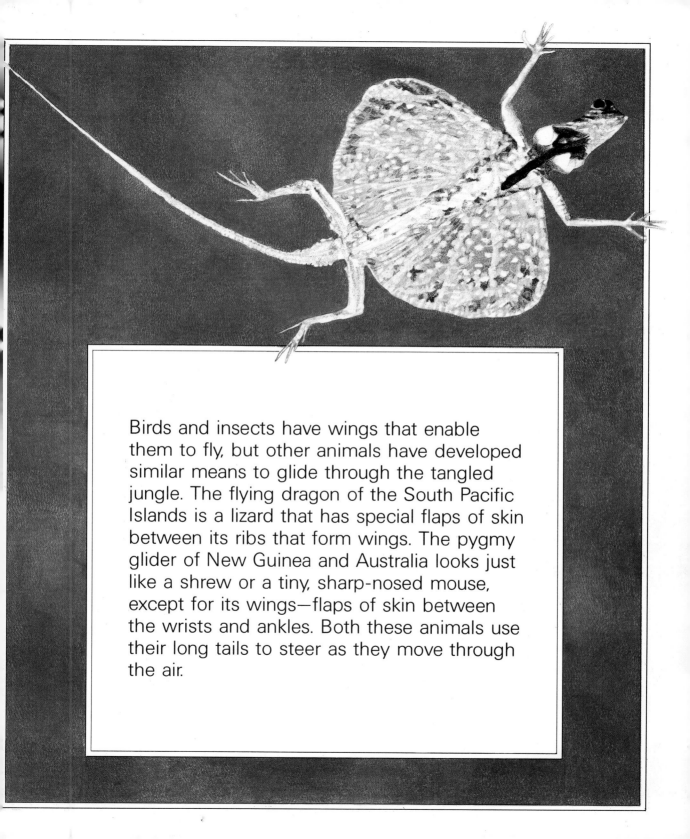

Birds and insects have wings that enable
them to fly, but other animals have developed
similar means to glide through the tangled
jungle. The flying dragon of the South Pacific
Islands is a lizard that has special flaps of skin
between its ribs that form wings. The pygmy
glider of New Guinea and Australia looks just
like a shrew or a tiny, sharp-nosed mouse,
except for its wings—flaps of skin between
the wrists and ankles. Both these animals use
their long tails to steer as they move through
the air.

The jungle is home to some of the world's deadliest snakes. One is the anaconda from the Amazon jungle—which is also the world's largest snake. Occasionally growing to over thirty feet, it kills birds and other animals by coiling around them and squeezing until the victim cannot breathe.

Poisonous snakes such as pit vipers have fangs that inject a deadly venom into the prey they bite. Even in the darkness of the jungle they can seek out victims by using special heat detectors on their heads. Their venom paralyzes and kills within minutes.

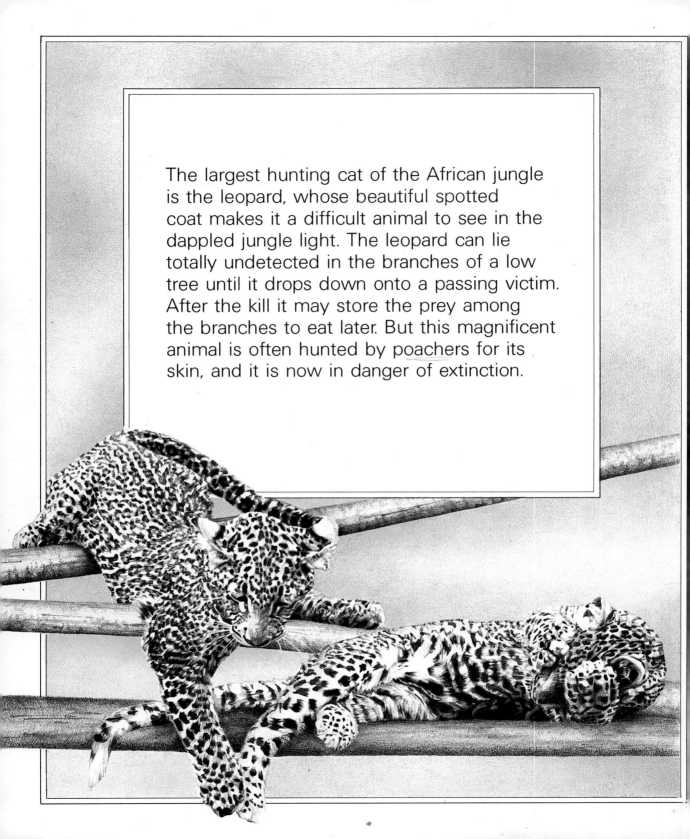

The largest hunting cat of the African jungle is the leopard, whose beautiful spotted coat makes it a difficult animal to see in the dappled jungle light. The leopard can lie totally undetected in the branches of a low tree until it drops down onto a passing victim. After the kill it may store the prey among the branches to eat later. But this magnificent animal is often hunted by poachers for its skin, and it is now in danger of extinction.

Monkeys and apes travel about the jungle with grace and agility. When moving through the trees, they cling to branches using their hands and feet. Perhaps the most acrobatic is the gibbon of Southeast Asia, which has enormously long arms that help it swing from tree to tree with incredible speed.

A gibbon in motion

South American monkeys such as the spider monkey have a fifth limb that clings—a long tail with a very strong grip. The tail can support the animal's entire weight. This gives it an extremely long reach and leaves its hands free to pick fruit from branches.

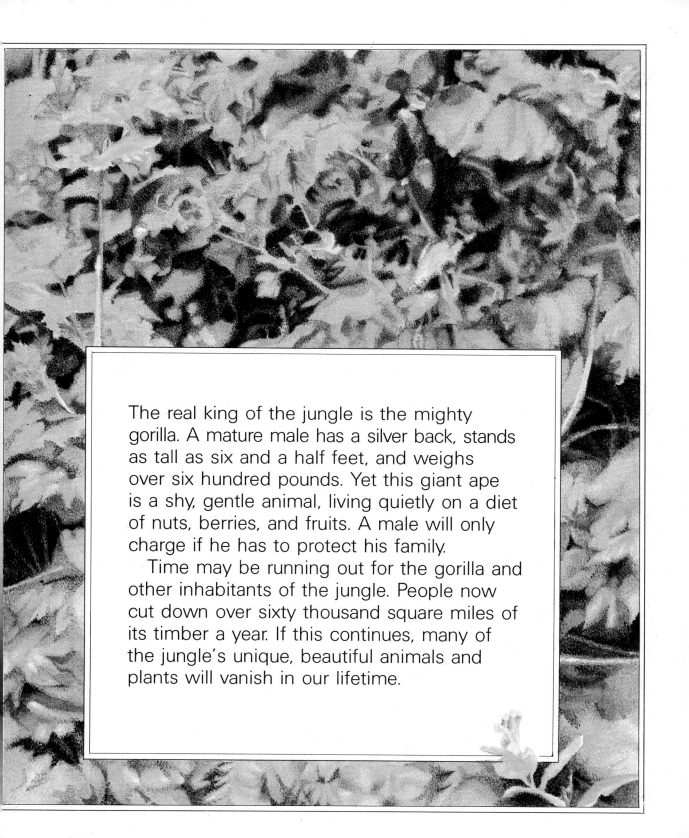

The real king of the jungle is the mighty gorilla. A mature male has a silver back, stands as tall as six and a half feet, and weighs over six hundred pounds. Yet this giant ape is a shy, gentle animal, living quietly on a diet of nuts, berries, and fruits. A male will only charge if he has to protect his family.

Time may be running out for the gorilla and other inhabitants of the jungle. People now cut down over sixty thousand square miles of its timber a year. If this continues, many of the jungle's unique, beautiful animals and plants will vanish in our lifetime.

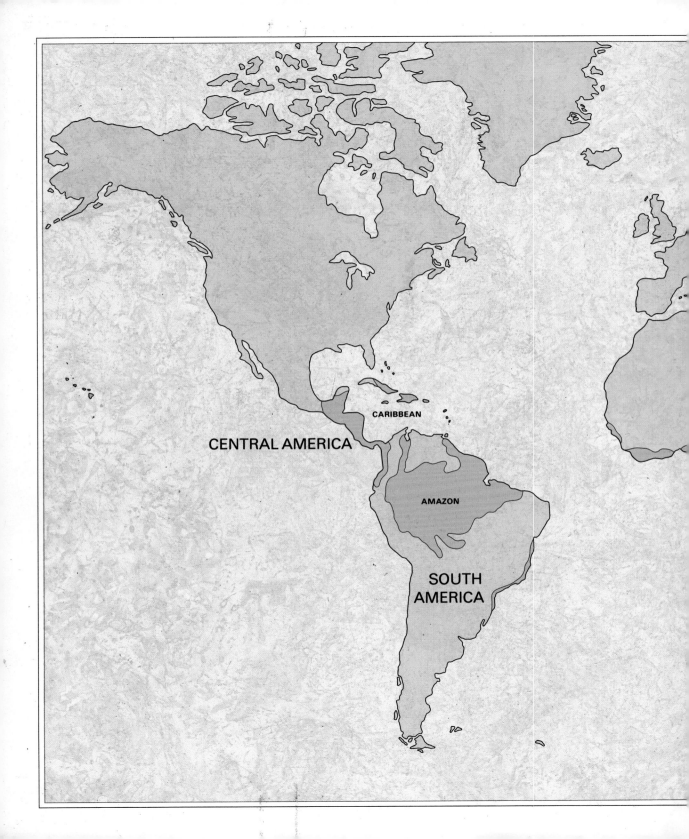